PSALMS OF MY LIFE

Psalms of My Life

JOSEPH BAYLY

LIFEJOURNEY
BOOKS

LifeJourney Books™ is an imprint of David C.
Cook Publishing Co.
David C. Cook Publishing Co., Elgin, Illinois
David C. Cook Publishing Co., Weston, Ontario
Nova Distribution Ltd., Newton Abbot, England

PSALMS OF MY LIFE
©1987 by the estate of Joseph Bayly

Cover design by Koechel/Peterson and Associates
First Printing, 1987
Printed in the United States of America
96 95 94 93 92   6 5 4 3 2
ISBN: 0-7814-0933-0
52811/A5224

ABOUT THE AUTHOR

After graduating from Wheaton College and Faith Theological Seminary, Joe Bayly's long career as author and educator began with his appointment to InterVarsity Christian Fellowship as a staff member to the Ivy League schools. Later he was editor of HIS magazine and the first director of InterVarsity Press, then joined the David C. Cook Publishing Company as managing editor, followed by positions as vice president for product and marketing, first vice president and finally president of the company.

For 25 years he wrote a column, "Out of My Mind," for *Eternity Magazine.* "Joe wrote with grace and good humor," says Russel Hitt, "but he was fearless in confronting Evangelicals about questionable practices, false piety, and pompous pretense." Shortly after writing a final silver anniversary column in July 1986, Joe joined three sons who preceded him in death.

He left behind his beloved wife of 43 years, Mary Lou, four children all involved in Christian service, and the Christian community of friends and people who were influenced toward holiness and Christian thinking by Joe's influence. Joe will be most remembered as a man of insight and wit, a person keenly sensitive both to the law of God and the needs of people. Writes one friend, "I loved being at the Bayly's—the mix of openness, honest, the cackling humor, the seriousness—and the feeling of freedom and an inner warmth of time well spent."

Indeed, Joe's life was a life well spent.

Two days ago
    You made the universe
    earth sun moon stars
    and everything
    including man
    praise God.
    Yesterday
    You lived among us
    shared our life
    taught healed and loved
    died for our sins
    rose from the dead
    praise God.
    Today You live in us
    who own You Lord
    praise God.
    Tomorrow You'll return
    to claim Your universe
    and rule
    and every knee
    in heaven and earth and under earth
    shall bow
    and every tongue confess
    that You
    are Lord
    praise God.

*Praise for
Four Days*

Thank You God
that You see
armies march
a sparrow fall
hear
atom's blast
a baby's cry
smell
volcano's flow
a man's sweat
feel
contour of mountains
a little lump
taste
ocean's salt
my tears.

A Psalm of
Praise

A Psalm of Heights & Depths

Praise the Lord.
    Praise Him in the Rockies
    riding mountain trails.
    Praise Him
    beside tumbling
    rushing
    rocky
    white capped stream.
    Praise Him
    in high meadow
    still forest.
    Praise Him on the Cape
    eating lobster, clams
    walking rainswept beach
    barefoot.
    Praise Him on Mount Baker
    holding ski rope
    going uphill
    then down.

Praise Him in the snowfall.
Praise Him in the lodge
sitting by the fire
looking out at stars.
Praise Him at the desk
phoning
writing
meeting
planning.
Praise Him in high places
and in low
in excitement
and monotony.
I will sing to the Lord
as long as I live.
I will be glad in the Lord
in the Lord.

Birthday Psalm

Tonight I'm fifty,
I've lived
for half a century
one twentieth
of a millennium.
One billion
eight hundred thirty-nine million
six hundred thousand
times
my heart has beat.
Eighteen thousand
two hundred fifty
times
I've gone to bed,
safe risen in the morning.
For this I thank you,
Lord who forgives,
Lord who heals
my sicknesses
and all my hurts.

Tonight I pray, Lord,
and every night to come
until night ends
and darkness flies away,
remind me of your mercy.
And then tomorrow,
when morning light returns,
and I arise
to love you, serve you,
remind me of your grace.
Listen, angels,
hosts of heaven,
listen servants of the Lord,
celebrate his work in me,
my blessings on his name.

A Psalm on Being Childlike

Lord, we're alone
for the first time
in more than three decades
We're alone.
No children home.
I said, "Lord
where is the way?"
You said, "I am
the way."
Lord of childhood
make me childlike
not childish
trusting
not scared
simple
not devious.
When you plow a field
Lord
I know you plan
a crop
when you harrow
breaking up plowed clods of dirt
to fine earth.

A Psalm in a Hotel Room

I'm alone Lord
alone
a thousand miles from home.
There's no one here who knows my
name
except the clerk
and he spelled it wrong
no one to eat dinner with
laugh at my jokes
listen to my gripes
be happy with me about what
happened today
and say that's great.
No one cares.

There's just this lousy bed
and slush in street outside
between the buildings.
I feel sorry for myself
and I've plenty of reason
to.
Maybe I ought to say
I'm on top of it
praise the Lord
things are great
but they're not.
Tonight
it's all
gray slush.

A Psalm about Self

Lord save me
from myself
my settled self
unsettle me
bring to end of rope
but only
if you
are at the end.
My procrastinating self
that can so easy find
side roads
that are more interesting
even ones where
errands can be run.
Send me back
to
my comfort loving self
uncomfort me
pull the covers from me
on cold night
that I may
wake. Starve my body
that my soul may feast.
My proud self.

Give me grace to bend myself
And keep me bent
lest you should
one day
bend me to the breaking point.
My righteous self
show me sin
that lurks beneath
my conscious thought
motivating
that pushes me
to settling
comfort pride
and self
rationalizing self
that finds excuse
for what I do
and don't.
Save me from myself
Save me so that
self may die
and save me
from pride
that self is dead.

A Psalm of Single Mindedness

Lord of reality
make me real
not plastic
synthetic
pretend phony
an actor playing out his part
hypocrite.
I don't want
to keep a prayer list
but to pray
nor agonize to find Your will
but to obey
what I already know
to argue
theories of inspiration
but submit to Your Word.

I don't want
to explain the difference
between eros and philos
and agape
but to love.
I don't want
to sing as if I mean it
I want to mean it.
I don't want
to tell it like it is
but to be it
like You want it.
I don't want
to think another needs me
but I need him
else I'm not complete.
I don't want
to tell others how to do it
but to do it
to have to be always right
but admit it
when I'm wrong.
I don't want
to be a census taker
but an obstetrician
nor an involved person
a professional

but a friend.
I don't want
to be insensitive
but to hurt
where other people hurt
nor to say
I know how you feel
but to say God knows
and I'll try
if you'll be patient with me
and meanwhile I'll be quiet.
I don't want
to scorn the clichés of others
but to mean everything I say
including this.

A Psalm of Dignity

Thank You
Lord Christ
for treating every other person
as an end
not a means
including me.
Thank You
that You never climbed
on other person's shoulders
never used a man or woman
boy or girl
as if he were a thing.
Thank You
for refusing to invade
the freedom
You have given us.
Thank You for refusing
to manipulate us
pressure us
maneuver us into a corner.
Thank You for treating us
as if we shared Your image.

A Psalm of the Fat Camel

This needle's eye
Lord
it is so very small
and I'm so very big
I can't squeeze through
not even little finger.
But then
I'm part of
the affluent society.
We've shown
as never people did before
how to get
acquire
build up
squander

and still get more
more things
cars houses
land rosebushes
money
stocks and bonds
more gross national product
and more defenses of it all
more of everything
this side of
needle's eye.
Lord have mercy.
Do a necessary miracle.

A Psalm of Forgetfulness

Lord
I'm becoming forgetful
names words
ideas
whether I did this or that.
Remind me Lord
of my memory.
Keep me sharp.
But if it ever
comes to that
let me forget
everything
except
Jesus loves me
this I know
for the Bible
tells me so
and
others love me
even if I forget
everything
including their names.

Psalm of a Gardener

Lord of the compost heap
you take garbage
and turn it into
soil good soil
for seeds to root
and grow
with wildest increase
flowers to bloom
with brilliant beauty.
Take all the garbage
of my life
Lord of the compost heap
turn it into
soil good soil
and then plant seeds
to bring forth
fruit and beauty
in profusion.

*S*ave me
God
from success.
I fear it
more than failure
which alerts me
to my nature
limitations
destiny.
I know that
any success
apart from Your Spirit
is mere euphemism
for failure.

A Psalm
When Things
Are Going Well

A Psalm
While Packing Books

This cardboard box
Lord
see it says
Bursting limit
200 lbs. per square inch.
The box maker knew
how much strain
the box would take
what weight
would crush it.
You are wiser
than the box maker
Maker of my spirit
my mind
my body.
Does the box know
when pressure increases close to
the limit?
No
it knows nothing.

But I know
when my breaking point
is near.
And so I pray
Maker of my soul
Determiner of the pressure
within
upon me
Stop it
lest I be broken
or else
change the pressure rating
of this fragile container
of Your grace
so that I may bear more.

A Psalm of Minor Miracles

Thank you
for what Deborah
calls minor miracles
Lord
like finding
a paper bag
a clean one
there on the sidewalk
ten steps after
you prayed for it
or going down
that awful
dirt road
on the side of the mountain
and only passing
four cars
in eight miles.

A Psalm of Memories

Lord
I smell fresh bread
just baked
mouth watering warm.
Lord, my mind goes back
mother kneading dough
taking loaf from pan
buttering a slice for me.
I smell trailing arbutus
sweet breath of mountain springtime
heavenly fragrance
I remember father
hands extended with arbutus
coming through the door
saying
Mary I found this

for you
in cinders
beside the railroad track
I smell baby powder
and hold again
a tiny infant now grown
our very own
smelling fresh, clean, human
as baby's mother
lifts him from the bath
Hands baby to me
and says, "Hold him, he's ours
our very own."
Lord thank you
for smells
that trigger memory
warm again with love.

A Psalm
of Desperation

God
hear my
silent
scream
say
peace
be still
to the storm
that rages
within me.

Lord you're the farmer
I'm your field
It is your right
to fence me in
to plow
my soul's hard ground
with furrows deep
to dig down far
for hidden rocks
to harrow hard
till soil is smooth
but only
if you plan
a harvest
of holiness.

*A Psalm
of Suffering*

A Psalm
of Personal Need

Lord, my heart is a ghetto
walled off
dark
depressed
danger filled
hurting.
Move in, Lord.
Renew it
renew my heart
destroy, burn
raze
remove.
Build it fresh
and then You live there.
You Lord.
Because then it'll stay
clean
pure
new.

A Psalm
of Obsession

In times of crisis
Lord
when we don't know
which way
the scales will tip
all else is
unimportant.
We couldn't care less about money
things
about what we eat
or whether.
We don't notice
rebuffs
comments that would ordinarily
disturb us.
Our mind is honed
to single edge.
You loom
above all else
fill our horizon.

Your will
becomes our food
our drink
the very air we breathe.
Too soon
the crisis passes
and we're back
where we were
before.
Dear Lord forgive.

I find it hard Lord
    agonizing hard
    to stand here
    looking through the glass
    at this my infant son.
    What suffering
    is in this world
    to go through pain of birth
    and then through
    pain of knife
    within the day.
    What suffering
    is in the world
    this never ending
    pain parade
    from birth
    to death.
    He moves
    a bit
    not much
    how could an infant
    stuffed with tubes
    cut sewed and bandaged
    move more than that?
    Some day he'll shout
    and run a race
    roll down a grassy hill

*A Psalm at
Children's
Hospital*

ice skate
on frosty night like this.
He'll sing and laugh
I know he will Lord.
But if not
if You should take him home
to Your home
help me then remember
how Your Son suffered
and You stood by
watching
agonizing watching
waiting
to bring all suffering to an end
forever
on a day
yet to be.
Look Lord
he sleeps.
I must go now.
Thank You for staying
nearer than oxygen
than dripping plasma
to my son.
Please be that near
to mother
sister brothers
and to me.

A Psalm on the Death of an Eighteen-Year-Old Son

What waste Lord
    this ointment precious
    here outpoured
    is treasure great
    beyond my mind to think.
    For years
    until this midnight
    it was safe
    contained
    awaiting careful use
    now broken
    wasted
    lost.

The world is poor
so poor it needs each drop
of such a store.
This treasure spent
might feed a multitude
for all their days
and then yield more.
This world is poor?
It's poorer now
the treasure's lost.
I breathe its lingering fragrance
soon even that
will cease.
What purpose served?
The act is void of reason
sense
Lord
madmen do such deeds
not sane.
The sane man hoards his treasure
spends with care
if good
to feed the poor
or else to feed himself.
Let me alone Lord
You've taken from me
what I'd give Your world.

I cannot see such waste
that You should take
what poor men need.
You have a heaven
full of treasure
could You not wait
to exercise Your claim
on this?
O spare me Lord forgive
that I may see
beyond this world
beyond myself
Your sovereign plan
or seeing not
may trust You
Spoiler of my treasure.
Have mercy Lord
here is my quitclaim.

A Psalm of Extremity

I cry tears
to you Lord
tears
because I cannot speak.
Words are lost
among my fears
pain
sorrows
losses
hurts
but tears
You understand
my wordless prayer
You hear.
Lord
wipe away my tears
all tears
not in distant day
but now
here.

🦌

Thank you Lord Jesus
that you're
not embarrassed
by serious illness
serious sin.
You don't draw back
afraid to speak
lest you say the wrong thing
afraid to touch
lest you become unclean tainted
too involved.
Thank you
that you bore these sins
these sicknesses and sorrows
you entered into
serious illness serious sin.

A Psalm about
Serious Illness

A Psalm in a Hospital Corridor

Lord
my heart fears.
I know that You have said
Fear not
but my heart fears.
Thoughts flash
across the track of my mind
thoughts of evil
not good
loss
not gain
suffering
not joy.
My thoughts are out of control.
They exhume the past
bury the future
make the present
a heavy heavy burden.
Lord
I cannot control
these fears these thoughts.
I cannot look at the future
with peace.
But I trust You.
These fears run wild

careering thoughts of evil
may make it seem
that I don't
but I do.
I trust You Lord.
I know Your thoughts toward me
are of good
not evil.
I fear evil
not You.
Yet fearing wild
I know that even evil
from Your hand
is purest good.
I fear
I trust.
I trust You Lord
I trust Your wisdom
life spanning
Your love
death taming.
I trust You
to know the end of this long beginning
moment.

A Psalm on Being

The little child says
Here I am daddy
as he bursts
on father's sight
from behind the chair
where he's been hiding.
He doesn't say
What can I do for you?
How can I help you?
I want to serve you
seeking somehow
to work and gain
the father's favor
and delight.
He knows that they are his
without exhausting effort
to achieve.
They are his always.
Here I am daddy
—Abba Father—
not working
just being
your eternal son.

*L*ord
if anything happens
if you come for me
keep them from interfering
desperately trying
to tug me
from your grasp.
If I'm far
across the river
where you own shore
and all beyond
don't let them
bring me back
prolonging death
not life
delaying life
that never crosses
unreturning river
again.

*A Psalm on
Viewing the River*

A Psalm of Awakening

Lord I want to die
in my sleep
I want to go to bed
and be awakened
by you
saying
Get up son
it's the first day of school
the beginning of your new job
the dawn of eternity.
Here are your clothes.
Your older brother
wore them first
now they're yours
forever
white and fresh and clean
smelling of heaven.

A Psalm for Christmas Eve

Praise God for Christmas
Praise Him for the Incarnation
for Word made flesh.
I will not sing
of shepherds watching flocks
on frosty night
or angel choristers.
I will not sing
of stable bare in Bethlehem
or lowing oxen
wise men
trailing distant star
with gold and frankincense and myrrh.
Tonight I will sing
praise to the Father
who stood on heaven's threshold
and said farewell to His Son

as He stepped across the stars
to Bethlehem
and Jerusalem.
And I will sing
praise to the infinite eternal Son
who became most finite
a Baby
who would one day be executed
for my crimes.
Praise Him in the heavens.
Praise Him in the stable.
Praise Him in my heart.

A Psalm of Christmas

Lord we blame
the innkeeper
for only giving you
the stable
when his inn was full
but what about
all the others
who lived in Bethlehem
that night
when you were born.
Why were
all their houses
that weren't full
of guests
fast closed
against the one
who contained you?
God bless
our little homes
this Christmastime

make them
big enough
to welcome you
contained in those
for whom the world
has no room
except
a cold and lonely
Christmas day.

King Jesus
why did you choose
a lowly ass
to carry you
to ride in your parade?
Had you no friend
who owned a horse
—a royal mount with spirit
fit for a king to ride?
Why choose an ass
small unassuming
beast of burden
trained to plow
not carry kings.

King Jesus
why did you choose
me
a lowly unimportant person
to bear you
in my world today?
I'm poor and unimportant
trained to work
not carry kings
—let alone the King of kings
and yet you've chosen me
to carry you in triumph

*A Psalm
for
Palm
Sunday*

in this world's parade.
King Jesus
keep me small
so all may see
how great you are
keep me humble
so all may say
Blessed is he who cometh in the name
of the Lord
not what a great ass he rides.

A Psalm for Maundy Thursday

Tonight
Lord Jesus Christ
You sat at supper
with Your friends.
It was a simple meal
that final one
of lamb
unleavened bread
and wine.
Afterward
You went out to die.
How many other meals You shared
beside the lake
fried fish and toasted bread
at Simon's banquet hall a feast
at Lazarus' home in Bethany

the meal that Martha cooked
on mountain slope
where You fed hungry crowd
at close of tiring day.
Please sit with us tonight
at our small meal
of soup and rolls and tea.
Then go with us
to feast of bread and win
that You provide
because afterward
You went out to die.

Let's celebrate Easter
with the rite
of laughter.
Christ died and rose
and lives.
Laugh like a woman
who holds her first baby.
Our enemy death
will soon be destroyed.
Laugh like a man
who finds he doesn't have cancer
or he does but now there's a cure.
Christ opened wide
the door of heaven.
Laugh like children
at Disneyland's gates.
This world is owned by God
and He'll return to rule.
Laugh like a man
who walks away uninjured
from a wreck
in which his car was totaled.
Laugh
as if all the people in the whole world
were invited to a picnic
and then invite them.

A Psalm for Easter

*A Psalm
on Moving
to Take a
New Job*

I take this step
Lord
in faith.
Faith that You
have confronted me
with this opening
Faith that You
have led me to accept
Faith that this change
will be a means
to great holiness
and love
to You
for me
my wife
our children
Faith
that You will make me
able for this new work
so that I may add
in every way
to what You
are already doing
where I go
Faith

that You will care
for mother sister
friends needy ones
we leave behind
Faith that You will make me
creative in my work
and in the exercise
of other gifts
Faith that by this change
You will make
life and self we share
my wife's and mine
and ours together
more real
more full
than it has been to now
Faith that this change
will bring much blessing
to each of our children
Faith in Your promise
that when You put forth
Your own sheep
You go before them.
Lord I will not go
unless You do this.

A Psalm of Appreciation for the New Church

This pew
is soft
cushioned.
Thank You Lord
for our new sanctuary
acoustically
near perfect
so we can hear
no matter how deaf
lighting
by an illumination engineer
so we can see
with even dimmest sight

air conditioned
so we can shut out
the heat
be cool
no matter what.
It's a great new sanctuary.
This soft pew
cushions me
against the wood.

A Psalm of Preaching

I'm on the bridge
Lord
the ship's bridge
steering shipload
of your people. There they are
on the deck looking up
trusting
scarcely knowing
of the icebergs
hidden reefs
wrecks of long gone ships
that I'm avoiding.
Keep me glued

to chart
that you've provided
to Holy Spirit's course
sensing dangers
most of all
the danger that I'll think
beyond the steering
I provide
power to make the ship move
on its appointed course.
Bring us all
to safe harbor
by twelve o'clock.

A Psalm on Spotting Sputnik 1957

See that speck
Lord
we put it there.
Not really us
Lord
the Russians did.
It shines so bright
as it passes
over Memorial Field
through darkling sky.
It is our evensong.
Whose sun does it reflect?
Why Yours
Lord.
Sputnik
is ours
the sun belongs to You.

Let me build a church
Lord
That's big enough for You.
Not big enough for them
or him or her
or me
but You.
Red door
open wide
high walls
enough to hem us in
to You
Your mind
windows without glass
through which
dove may fly
steeple
rising rising
through low clouds
to sky
and star beyond
tolling death
pealing life.

*A Psalm of
Church
Building*

A Psalm of
Appreciation for Music

Thank You for music
Lord
Handel and Haydn Society
and Boston Symphony
present
Handel's Messiah.
He shall feed His flock
like a shepherd
shall gather the lambs with His arm
and carry them in His bosom.
Students on Fairview Island
singing
Who is on the Lord's side

who will serve the King?
Mother holding little boy
rocking
humming
All through the night
my Savior will be watching
and Like a river glorious
is God's perfect peace.
Little group of people
before an open grave
singing
Jesus I love Thee
and up from the grave He arose.

A Psalm of Thanksgiving
for a Christian Bookstore

Thank you, Lord
   for this store
   where bread is sold
   to feed the soul.
   Not stones
   that after they have failed
   to quiet hunger
   break the teeth
   or serpents
   that pretend to satisfy
   the frightful lust
   of one who eats
   and then
   administer
   the sting of death.

   But bread from heaven
   via Bethlehem
   that House of Bread
   where one night's toil
   produced enough
   to feed a starving world
   of souls
   through all of time

and via Calvary
where bread was broken
to arise afresh
and fill the world
with warm aroma
of loaf
fresh baked
life giving
death halting.

Can any store
put out this bread
for sale?
No, bread of life
is without price
and anyone who hungers
has it free.
Containers only
are for sale
to take it home
and eat
or feed another.

Thank you Lord
for this store
where bread is sold
to feed the soul.

A Psalm in a Colorado Meadow

Twenty wild flowers Lord
no twenty-two.
Here they are
all round where I sit
waiting.
I don't know their names
except arbutus
trailing arbutus
and daisies.
Maybe I could give names
to the rest.
Blue glory in the morning
or blue funk
yellow elf
Aunt Elizabeth's prayerbook
Job's tears
there are a lot of them Lord
all over the meadow.
Lonely gumdrop
the purple kind
that's left in the dish
when all the rest are gone.

Mouse corsage
gopher's hay.
Pink pumps of pinkelumps
Sergeant Pepper's epaulets
Eleanor Rigby's shroud.
Let's see
did I name that one
or those?
I've lost track.
The rest will be nameless
because here come the children
running through the stream
back from climbing
their stone mountain.
Thank You for wild flowers
Lord
mountains
rushing streams
children
each different.
Thank You.

A Psalm on
TWA Flight 81

High above the clouds
six miles over earth
I think of Time
and Life
not timeless life
or coffee tea or milk
not living water
bread of life
of landing
on hard concrete strip
not flying on
to meet You.
I guess I fear that.
Earthbound in the heavens
Lord
not heavenbound.
Lord have mercy.

This ghost town
Lord
once live
now dead
boarded up
against the world
the flesh
the devil.
The devil? No
he lives here
in shuttered house
abandoned mine
boarded post office
tavern store.
He's at home
in ghost town
not town alive
with children
hammers
violins.

*A Psalm
of St. Elmo
Colorado*

A Psalm of Bear Trap Revisited in the Fall

Lord, I see the aspen
stand out gold
among the green and gray
of mountains round.
It takes the fall
to isolate them
set them stark
defined
they can
no longer hide.
Twenty summers ago
Lord
We planted trees
here
in Brown Bear
Pooh Bear
Three Bears Polar Bear
Lodge
Cook House
Bear's Den
and this log
on sunny afternoon
here
where I sit.

Now fall has come
and some stand
tall and gold
amid encircling pines.
Others are small
too short to see
distinguish from
the gray and green
A few though still alive have died
while other few
alive
though dead
have grown beyond
the mountains
mist
and sky.
You cannot hide
an aspen
planted on
rocky mountain
when fall comes.
I wonder about the trees
they're planting
summers now.

A Psalm in
Mojave Desert

I said
  this desert land is barren
  void of life and beauty.
  I drive for miles
  see nothing
  only sand and sage
  feel nothing
  only wind and heat
  taste nothing
  but spit dried spit.

He said
have you ever driven
in spring
through this same desert
seen blossoms flower
gorgeous wild?
It's all a thing of timing.
Seeds of beauty
are there now hidden
waiting fall of rain
to bring them life.
Lord send rain
upon my world
my life
I'm tired of dried spit.

I will praise the Lord
for communications media.
For printed page
that says
a hundred thousand times
God loves you.
Here's the answer
to your problem
question doubt need.
For radio broadcast
television program
that enters in
where doors are closed
blinds drawn
homes without number
cars
hospital wards
prison cells
barracks
dormitory rooms
and says
You're not alone.
God loves you.
He'll meet you here
and now.

*A Psalm of
Meaning
Exchange*

You needn't go out
to strange church
crowded meeting hall.
For records tapes
Braille books
that tell the blind
God loves you.
I will praise the Lord
for communications media.
I will praise the Lord
for a man
a woman
who grasps trembling hand
under oxygen tent
who sits on edge
of barracks bed
who looks the prisoner
in the eye
who buys a Coke for student
who walks with blind
and says
God loves you
and they know
he does
too.

A Psalm of Thanksgiving for Leaders

Thank You for our leaders
for pastors
who feed us
serve us and our children
as Your ministers
Son of God
who came not to be served
but to serve
for theologians
who give us answers
questions
reasons for our hope
from Your Word
Father of Lights

for evangelists
who harvest the field
You have brought
to fruition
Holy Spirit
for teachers
who make us think
of You
ourselves and others
because You have taught them.
Thank You for our leaders
Your followers.

A Psalm in Celebration of Missionaries

How happy are those
who take the Gospel
to other lands.
They obey Your command
Lord Jesus
Your command to tell
the Good News
everywhere
to every person
in the whole world.
They forsake
kindred and friends
houses and land
comfort security things
to go tell
teach
heal
love.

They are the great ones
of this generation
of whom the world
is not worthy.
They are the ones
whom the world pities.
Poor world.
Poor pitiful world.
They are Your ambassadors
sent by You
to declare an end
to hostility
and announce peace
through Your death
and endless life.
How happy are those
who take the Gospel
to other lands.

A Psalm of Praise for the Tribes

I will sing
   of the tribes of earth
   who have turned
   from darkness
   to light
   not flickering dying campfire
   but sun of opening day.
   Walamo
   Kambatta Hadiya
   Yoruba
   Mixtec Tzeltal Cakchiquel
   Shapras Aucas
   Lisu Katu
   Picts
   Angles Saxons Swabians
   Visigoths.

I will sing
of men and women
who brought light
to the tribes.
Ohman Bergsten
Crouch
Pike Slocum Townsend
Cox and Anderson
The five who died
Elisabeth Elliot
Rachel Saint
Fraser
Smith
Boniface Willibrand
Ulfilas.
I will sing
of the Light
of earth's tribes
who will shine in them
forever.

A Psalm of the Young Pastor

Lord
the grass is dry
brown drying
Send rain I ask
refreshing, renewing
reviving rain
an all day rain
that gets down to its roots
so that it will live
again
be green
cool to my feet
Lord
my soul is dry
send rain
down to my roots
so that I may be cool
to your feet

A Psalm of a
Weary Prophet

Lord, I'm a weary prophet
You're a prophet?
Even that word
using it for myself
shows my weary state.
You're no Jeremiah
—forgive me
for inveighing like one.
Nor Jonah
—except in the belly
of the great fish.
Nor Amos
—I'm the one
to whom that man spoke.
Maybe I'm just
a common scold
iconoclast
(that sounds better)
critic
controversialist
prophet

—there
I said it again
Who am I
to question
doctrine
manners morals
A voice.
Then let others speak
You'll never be a prophet
but you can speak for me
—like Balaam's ass.

A Psalm of a Seminary Wife

Books I hate you
    hate your claims
    upon my husband
    hiding there behind your covers
    instead of under mine.
    Who ever thought that I'd
    play second fiddle
    to a book?

Typewriter I hate you
    typing papers
    typing thesis
    footnotes, quotes
    diaphoresis.
    Who ever thought that I'd be
    secretary
    to my mate?

Apartment I hate you
    hate the room
    where babies
    and cries

disturbing
other tenants
and my husband
as he studies all the time.

Meals I hate you
hate the pennies
I am watching
as I serve
by light of candle
gourmet macaroni dishes
to my educated husband
on the run.

Job I hate you
hate the way
my husband's growing
in his knowledge and becoming
educated more and more
while I'm tied to
stupid repetitions
rote of work.

Husband I hate you
hate your easy
expectation
that I'm free from all emotion

keeping children
from commotion
so that you
can study all the time.

Tears I hate you
hate the way
you come unbidden
when he fails
to hug or kiss me
and when he forgets
to pray or read the Bible unassigned.

God I love you.
Are you surprised
I know I'd be
if someone griped of situation
thought I'd planned their deprivation
when my plan
by love conceived
was for their total good.

A Psalm for a Nurse

Father
I'm a nurse
and patients are enough
to keep me busy
every hour of my day
or night.
But that's not all.
There are the relatives beside
and doctors
orderlies and aides
other nurses too
the chaplain
with all kinds and shapes of clergymen
and topping all the heap
director and administrator
who run the hospital itself
and me.

Father
I am weak
but others lean on me
I am tired
but others need my strength
I'm alone
full conscious of my solitary life

yet thrust into the hurting circles
of families facing loss.
Father make me competent
a nurse who knows just what to do
in an emergency
at three a.m.
when no one is around
but me.
I want to be a good nurse
the sort that parents trust
with infant treasure
in neonatal care
when they must leave at night.
The sort that senses pain
or fear of pain,
or fear of loss
—of breast of sight
of life itself—
and sensing
shares the word or touch
that turns them from their fears
to you.

Father make me real
a person helping others
without power sick dying
but values far beyond
the hospital itself.

Make me real
not empty uniform
that moves from room to room,
mechanical and cold.
I need your warmth
your love for people
yes for those
who argue in the E.R.
beside the still cold body of their son
about responsibility
for accident or overdose that killed.
I need your warmth
in operating room
toward doctor as he curses
at my clumsiness
my inability to read his mind.
I need your warmth
toward patients who complain
who signal for attention all the time
especially the ones
who aren't as sick
as some who never ask for help.

I need your peace
when face to face with death
unable to do more than hold a hand
and watch.

I feel so helpless
many times.
What good is all my skill
before this awful foe?
I need your balance
lest I become obsessed with death
disease and pain
and think the whole world's sick
including me.
How easily I diagnose
the symptoms of my illness
doubtless fatal.
Help me to turn from pain's parade
to joyful life
from sickness to the world of health
from charts and sterile tubes and medicines
to family and friends
to bundled children
playing in the snow
without guilt
that I am well
that I can run and see my breath
and eat a dinner out
with candles
and the one I love.

A Psalm on a Cold Night

Lord thank you
for this warm presence
here lying at my side
in holy dark.
Thank you
for beauty
present from the start
refined by sufferings
and joys
of forty years.
Thank you
for pureness, patience
faith and courage
love
that mounted
in crescendo
drums and cymbals
now muted quiet
flute and strings
and tiny bells.

Thank you
that turning over
I am warmed
and comforted
by this long burning fire.
She grasps my hand
and squeezes in her sleep.
Tonight Lord
thank you
for that wonder
that what you joined together
no woman man
or hell itself
could sunder.

A Psalm of Love

Thank you for children
brought into being
because we loved.
God of love
keep us loving
so that they
may grow up whole
in love's overflow.

Lord Christ
You loved the poor.
It was a sign
that You were who
You claimed to be.
You bothered
with them
preached to them
invited to be rich and full.
Forgive me Lord
for falling short
of such a love as Yours
that broke through crust
of poverty
for beggar
like me.

🦁

*A Psalm of
Poverty*

A Psalm of Mystery

You made known Your ways
to Moses
God
Your acts
to his people Israel.
They only saw
the sea divide
and swallow Pharaoh's host
the fire by night
the cloud by day.
They tasted manna
quail
drank water from the rock.
It was enough
for them to live
by what You did
leave reason to another.

Not Moses
he was a different sort
who prayed
Show me now
Your ways O God.
And You did.
You let him see
the principles
behind Your acts
and past the principles
the character displayed
eternal character
that forms the principles
the acts
and all.
Make me a Moses
God
dissatisfied with all things
short of You.

A Psalm of Faith

Thunder
crashing roaring
wakens me.
I get up
to close the window
against the rain.
Lightning tears the sky
for fragmentary moment
I see the yard
wheelbarrow
trees road field
and distant hill.
All is dark again
I return to sleep.
Thank You for the storm
that wakens me
and lightning flash
illumining
things near and far
in usual dark.

I plead guilty
Lord
I stand
awaiting
sentence
my crimes
spread out before You
Just Judge
of all the earth
I have no words
to lessen guilt.
No other can I blame
distant Adam
near people
except myself.
My guilt I bear
alone.
Alone?
Another stood alone
before You
and took my sentence
Lord.
Now I am free
to praise you
Just Judge
to please You
Criminal in my place.

*A Psalm of
Forgiveness*

A Psalm
about the
Shortness
of Life

I said
O Lord
let me end the work
You gave to me to do.
So much
must yet be done
before the dark
so little time
remains
before I'm home.
You are eternal
God

a thousand years to You
is but a passing day.
You scatter ages
I hoard my hours.
Please understand
my need for time
to do Your will
complete my job.
I understand
He said
I do
I only had
three years
of days
and I was through.

A Psalm
Requesting Faith

Give me courage Lord
    to take risks
    not the usual ones
    respected
    necessary
    relatively safe
    but those I could avoid
    the go for broke ones.
    I need courage
    not just because
    I may fall on my face
    or worse
    but others seeing me
    a sorry spectacle
    if it should happen
    will say
    he didn't know what he was doing
    or he's foolhardy
    or he's old enough to know

you lead from the side
instead of letting yourself be caught
in wild stampede.
Give me courage Lord
to take unnecessary risks
live at tension
instead of opting out.
Give me the guts to put up
instead of shutting up.
When it comes right down to it
Lord
I choose to be Your failure
before anyone else's success.
Keep me from reneging
on my choice.

A Psalm of World and Life

Lord give me a view
of this world
and this life
the sort that comes
when you climb a mountain
a hill
or even go out
on a rooftop.
I want to see things from above
from your perspective
not from beneath.
I want to see
you at work
in history including
the evening news
nature's beauty
nature's terror
science space
the church in history
and today.

I want to see
your image
shine through music, art,
drama, books.
But most of all
let me view
my life
from above
see goals, priorities,
achievements, failures
from your perspective.
O Lord
burn eternity
into my eyeballs.

A Psalm to the God Man

Lord Jesus Christ
I thank you
that you were real
a real man
and before that
a real boy.
It hurt
when you were planing wood
and you got a splinter
under your nail.
You felt it
when a stone got stuck
in your sandal.
You had to shake it out.
You removed the sand
from between your toes
and slept on hard ground
on cold night
dreaming of foxes
with their warm holes.
You got thirsty
hungry
tired
bone tired
tired of crowds
tired because you walked
too far.
You died.
Lord Jesus Christ

I thank you
that you were real
real God.
You healed people's hurts
even raised their dead.
You said
Come to me
if you're tired
and I will give you rest.
You fed hungry crowds
and said
I am living bread
that came down from heaven.
You rose from deadness
into life bringing life.
Lord Jesus Christ
I thank you
that you were real
real God man.
I worship you
I adore you
because you who bore
my sins
know what it's like
to have a splinter
under your nail
and to die.

A Psalm of Wandering

Lord You know
I'm such a stupid sheep.
I worry
about all sorts of things
whether I'll find grazing land
still cool water
a fold at night
in which I can feel safe.
I don't.
I only find troubles
want
loss.

I turn aside from You
to plan my rebel way.
I go astray.
I follow other shepherds
even other stupid sheep
Then when I end up
on some dark mountain
cliffs before
wild animals behind
I start to bleat
Shepherd Shepherd
find me save me
or I die.
And You do.

A Psalm of Assurance

I said
    Lord give me assurance
    that I'm really saved.
    I find doubt
    uncertainty
    so easy
    I want to feel
    consistently
    I'm justified
    just as if I'd never sinned
    pardoned
    sure of gaining heaven.
    He said
    Isn't my word
    enough?
    I've promised
    you will never perish
    you're held in my hand
    and in my father's hand.
    Can life eternal
    ever end?

Will any father
desert
child he loves?
Yes some would
but would I
loving you with
everlasting love?
When birth comes
from above
can you go back
into the womb?
Why seek more
believe less
than I have promised?
I shall never leave you
nor forsake you.
Will I ever abandon
the sheep I found
and brought back
to the fold?

A Psalm of Today

This is the day
the Lord has made.
The Lord?
Today?
Yesterday perhaps
could claim Your craft
or hopefully tomorrow
but not today
this disappointing day so filled
with problems
needs
despair and doubt.
This is the day
the Lord has made
and making it
He'll give me strength
and hope
to take me through.
This is the day
the Lord has made
so I'll be glad
and I'll rejoice in it.

*L*ord Christ
Your servant
Martin Luther
said he only had
two days
on his calendar
today
and that day
and that's
what I want too.
and I want
to live
today
for
that day.

*A Psalm of
Anticipation*

Joe's love for his wife, love for his family, and love for his God filled his life. So we conclude this wonderful collection with a poem he lovingly inscribed to Mary Lou on the back of a Mother's Day card just a few years ago.

To M.L.
Mother's Day,
1982

—to celebrate your creation of children
What a Holy Spirit calling:
To create an infant
within yourself
Your very inmost self—Nourish, protect, prepare
Then bring to birth
Nurse, feed
—run between stove and table in teenage—
Teach, discipline, hope, expect
Love
And all the while pray
with faith in God
Bring to safe harbor
through calm and storm
and monstrous waves
to wholeness
and useful life
on earth
in heaven
    That God should call
    three to live and serve there
    four to live and serve here
What a calling!

                     Your Joe

OTHER BOOKS BY JOSEPH BAYLY

The Last Thing We Talk About

Heaven

The Gospel Blimp and other Modern Parables

Winterflight